Reduce, Reuse, Recycle

Metal

Alexandra Fix

Heinemann Library
Chicago, Illinois

Customer Service 888-454-2279
Visit our website at www.heinemannraintree.com

Designed by Steven Mead and Debbie Oatley
Printed in China by South China Printing Company Limited

12 11 10 09 08
10 9 8 7 6 5 4 3 2

ISBN 10-digit: 1-4034-9717-6 (hc) 1-4034-9725-7 (pb)

Library of Congress Cataloging-in-Publication Data
Fix, Alexandra, 1950-
 Metal / Alexandra Fix.
   p. cm. -- (Reduce, reuse, recycle)
 Includes bibliographical references and index.
 ISBN 978-1-4034-9717-8 (hc) -- ISBN 978-1-4034-9725-3 (pb)
 1. Metals--Recycling--Juvenile literature. 2. Scrap metals--Recycling--Juvenile literature. 3. Metal products--Juvenile literature. I. Title.
 TS214.F56 2007
 669.028'6--dc22
                        2007002785

Acknowledgments
The author and publisher are grateful to the following for permission to reproduce copyright material: Alamy pp. **7** (Leslie Garland Picture Library), **10** (Tom Payne), **15** (Imagebroker), **20** (Megapress), **21** (Nic Hamilton); Ardea pp. **9** (David Hancock), **25** (Jean Michel Labat); Corbis pp. **5** (Matt Rainey/Star Ledger), **8** (James L. Amos), **11** (Yang Liu), **12** (Latour Stephanie), **13** (Cheryl Diaz Meyer/Dallas Morning News), **14** (André Fichte/Zefa), **23** (James L. Amos), **26** (Peter Beck), **27** (O. Alamany & E. Vicens), **28** (Lane Kennedy); Getty Images p. **19** (Photodisc Red); NHPA p. **4** (ANT Photo Library); Photolibrary.com pp. **6**, **16** (Plain Picture), **17** (Banana Stock), **18** (Phototake Inc.); Science Photo Library pp. **22** (Alex Bartel), **24** (Rosenfeld Images Ltd.).

Cover photograph reproduced with permission of Corbis/Douglas Whyte.

Every effort has been made to contact copyright holders of any material reproduced in this book. Any omissions will be rectified in subsequent printings if notice is given to the publisher.

Contents

Some words are shown in bold, **like this**. You can find out what they mean by looking in the glossary.

What Is Metal Waste?

People use metal every day. We ride in cars and buses made of metal, drink juice from metal cans, and use metal forks and knives. Metal is an important material, but sometimes it is wasted.

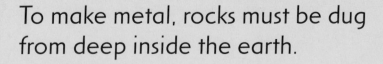

To make metal, rocks must be dug from deep inside the earth.

Metal drink cans can be recycled.

Metal waste is metal that is thrown away.
If metal is reused or **recycled**, it can be
used over and over again. This would
waste less metal.

What Is Made of Metal?

Many different items are made of metal. We use metal to make small items such as paperclips and soda cans. We use it to make large things such as cars, bridges, and buildings.

Today most airplanes are made of metal.

Metal cans store fruits, vegetables, and soups.

Homes are filled with metal items, such as canned foods. We often cover food with foil and cook with metal pans.

Where Does Metal Come From?

Metal comes from rocks **mined** from the ground. Metal is removed from the rocks by heating and melting them.

Rocks that make metal are dug from the ground.

Bauxite is used to make aluminum.

The two most common metals are aluminum and steel. Aluminum comes from a rock called bauxite. Steel is made from iron ore rock and carbon. Carbon comes from coal.

Will We Always Have Metal?

This ship is carrying iron ore.

Aluminum is a **nonrenewable resource**. Once this material is used up, it will be gone forever.

10

Steel is made from two nonrenewable resources: iron ore and coal. Coal is in shorter supply than iron ore and aluminum.

Steel is made by heating iron ore with coal.

What Happens When We Waste Metal?

Metal waste is harmful to the **environment**. Some metal waste is buried in **landfills**. It may take hundreds of years for the metal to break down.

Animals can get injured by metal that has rusted.

Old aluminum cans break down into tiny metal pieces. These pieces can kill fish.

Steel is a type of metal that slowly breaks down and creates a powdery dust called **rust**. Rust then enters the soil. It can get into nearby rivers and lakes and cut off sunlight to plants. This causes plants, fish, and tiny water creatures to die.

How Can We Reduce Metal Waste?

The best way to reduce metal waste is to use less metal. Instead of buying drinks in metal cans, take a reusable drink container with you.

Mix drinks in a pitcher at home.

→

Buying fresh fruits and vegetables reduces metal waste from canned foods.

Buy fresh food whenever possible. Canned foods waste metal. If you do use food packaged in cans, buy larger cans. One large can wastes less metal than two small cans.

How Can We Reuse Metal?

You can reduce metal waste by reusing metal. Share things made of metal with someone else. Give away bikes and toys that you no longer use.

Try to fix broken things instead of throwing them away.

Wash foil pans and use them again. ↑

You can also reuse small metal items for art projects. Make new containers by decorating used metal cans with paper or paint. These can hold your pencils, pens, crayons, or small toys.

How Can We Recycle Metal?

↑ Spray cans should be emptied but not squashed.

When metal is **recycled**, it is melted down and used again to make a new item. Most **communities** have a recycling program for metal, paper, plastic, and glass.

18

After you have saved metal items, get them ready for recycling. First remove plastic lids and rinse out cans. Ask an adult to flatten aluminum cans.

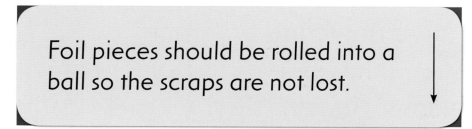

Foil pieces should be rolled into a ball so the scraps are not lost.

Where Can We Bring Metal for Recycling?

Some places have **recycling** programs. People can leave items in recycling bins near their garbage cans. A recycling truck picks up the recycled items at each home.

Recycling trucks bring materials to recycling centers.

Recycling centers have areas where you can sort different materials for recycling.

If your **community** does not have a recycling program, you can bring used beverage cans to a grocery store. From there they are brought to a recycling center.

How Is Metal Recycled?

At a **recycling** center, aluminum is separated from steel. Then the metals are packed into large bundles, called bales. At the metal **factory**, bales are chopped into tiny pieces.

This large magnet picks up metal from other waste. ↑

The pieces are melted in a **furnace** to turn the metal into liquid. After the liquid metal is removed from the furnace, it cools and hardens. The hardened metal is rolled out flat to use for new products.

Melted aluminum is poured and hardened into bars called ingots.

How Do We Use Recycled Metal?

Recycled metal can be used over and over again. Heavy steel can be reused to make car bodies, roofs, and small **appliances** such as toaster ovens.

These sheets of steel will be used to make new items.

Sheets of recycled steel can be used to make food cans.

Old aluminum beverage cans are often recycled into the same thing. Foil wrappers can become wrappers again.

How Can You Take Action?

You can help reduce metal waste. Ask family and friends to start **recycling** metal. You can help by rinsing out cans for recycling.

A good school project could be setting up a recycling container outside the school cafeteria.

Ask your teacher if your class can start recycling beverage and food cans. Find out where your local recycling station is located. By reducing our own metal waste, we can help keep our planet clean.

Make a Tin Can Telephone

Ask an adult to help you with this project.

Tin can telephones work in a similar way to real telephones. The vibrations of your voice travel down the tight string into the other can.

Follow these steps to make your own tin can telephone:

1. Wash out two metal cans.
2. Ask an adult to punch a hole into the bottom of each can.
3. Cut a piece of string about 5 yards (4.6 meters) long.
4. Thread the string through each can and tie a knot at the ends.
5. Find a friend. Walk as far apart as you can so you stretch the string tight.
6. Hold the can to one person's ear while the other person talks into the can. Take turns talking and listening.

Glossary

appliance household machine, such as a dishwasher or toaster, that usually runs on electricity or gas

community group of people who live in one area

environment natural surroundings for people, animals, and plants

factory building or buildings where something is made

furnace closed-off space that is heated at high temperatures to warm a building or melt solid materials

landfill large area where trash is dumped, crushed, and covered with soil

mine dig out a material that lies deep in the earth

nonrenewable resource material of the earth that cannot be replaced by nature

recycle break down a material and use it again to make a new product. Recycling is the act of breaking down a material and using it again.

rust reddish-brown coating that forms when iron or steel starts to break down

Find Out More

Books to Read

Galko, Francine. *Earth Friends at Home.* Chicago: Heinemann Library, 2004.

Kras, Sara Louise. *Metal.* Mankato, MN: Capstone Press, 2004.

Oxlade, Chris. *How We Use Metal.* Chicago: Raintree, 2005.

Web Sites

The Environmental Protection Agency works to protect the air, water, and land. The organization has a special Web site for students at <u>www.epa.gov/kids.</u>

Earth911 is an organization that gives information about where you can recycle in your community. Their Web site for students is <u>http://www.earth911.org/master. asp?s=kids&a=kids/kids.asp</u>.

Index